AF697223

Air Transportation Regulatory Reform

American Enterprise Institute for Public Policy Research
Washington, D.C.

KF
2439.3
.A45

ISBN 0-8447-0207-2
Legislative Analysis No. 25, 95th Congress
1 March 1978

Price $2.00 per copy

CONTENTS

INTRODUCTION

The Civil Aeronautics Board (CAB) is responsible for the economic regulation of the U.S. airline industry.[1] Since 1958, the Federal Aviation Administration (FAA)[2] has been independently responsible for air safety regulation. The CAB is empowered to determine which firms may engage in interstate air transportation, what routes they may serve, and what fares they may charge. In addition, it may distribute subsidies, and all airline mergers and intercarrier agreements are subject to CAB approval.

In recent years, CAB regulation, as well as other types of government regulation, has been the subject of increasing criticism from public officials, consumer groups, academic economists, and others. These critics contend that existing CAB regulation, instituted when the airline industry was in its formative stages, is inappropriate for the modern U.S. air transportation system. They argue that the limited experience with reduced regulation, such as that on intrastate routes, indicates that consumers and air carriers would be better served by a relaxation of CAB regulation.

Proposals to reform regulation of the airlines have included the Ford administration's proposed Aviation Act of 1975 and the bills emanating from hearings conducted by Senators Edward Kennedy (D-Mass.) and Howard Cannon (D-Nev.), by Congressman Glenn Anderson (D-Calif.), and by others. The focus of this analysis is legislation introduced in the Senate and House of Representatives in 1977, primarily S. 2493 and H.R. 8813. Both the Senate version (S. 2493, Sen. Cannon), referred to the Committee on Commerce, Science and Transportation, and the House version (H.R. 8813, Rep. Anderson and others), referred to the Committee on Public Works and Transportation, are amendments to the Federal Aviation Act of 1958, the main statutory basis for CAB regulation.

The Senate and House bills contain numerous provisions intended to alter CAB regulation. The most significant changes would affect airline regulation in five major areas: (1) general policy of the Board; (2) certification of new air carriers; (3) award of new routes to existing carriers; (4) flexibility of air fares; and, (5) reduction or suspension of air service.

Underlying the debate over the Senate and House bills is the issue of airline deregulation. Arguments concerning the desirability of legislative changes depend directly on the validity of assertions that airline service would be more efficient in a deregulated climate. The reason is that both bills represent limited steps in the direction of deregulation of the passenger airline industry. Thus, discussion of the extreme positions of deregulation versus the status quo will serve to place the Senate and House bills in perspective.

Opponents argue that competition is unworkable in the airline industry, and would result in route abandonments, predatory pricing, airline monopolies, and reduced air safety. Proponents assert that competition would bring about new types of service, lower fares, greater efficiency, and reasonable profits for air carriers.

At issue, in the bills currently under consideration and in this analysis, is passenger air transportation only. In the closing days of the first session of the 95th Congress, the House and Senate approved and President Carter signed H.R. 6010 into law as P.L. 95-163 providing for limited deregulation of the air-cargo industry. Under the terms of the law, one year after enactment any U.S. citizen may apply to the CAB to operate an all-cargo air service, and the CAB will be required to issue a certificate within 180 days unless the Board finds the applicant not "fit, willing, and able" to provide the service. Rates for air cargo service will be much more flexible, although they are not totally deregulated.

This analysis begins by analyzing specific provisions of the proposed legislation and then presents the major arguments for and against airline deregulation.

PENDING LEGISLATION

The main provisions of the primary Senate and House airline regulatory reform bills are presented below. This legislation usually strikes a middle position between complete deregulation and maintenance of the existing CAB regulatory program. One provision of the Senate bill is designed to deal with the possible results of deregulation of the passenger airline industry. This is section twenty-two, creating an employee protection program, which will guarantee that airline employees who lose their jobs because of the change of regulatory structure of the airline industry effected by this bill, will not suffer a reduction in salary. Monthly assistance payments, under this program, may extend for thirty-six months, but will be reduced by an amount equal to any unemployment compensation received by the former employee. Accompanying the detailed analysis of the major provisions of the bills are tables showing the existing law and the changes each bill would make.

Overall CAB Policy

Existing Law	S. 2493	H.R. 8813
Directs the CAB to promote adequate, economical, and efficient air service, relying on competition to the extent necessary to achieve goals.	Directs the CAB to maintain a system relying on actual and potential competition among air carriers.	Directs the CAB to rely on competitive market forces to determine the nature and price of air service.

Both the Senate and the House bills mandate changes in the CAB's declaration of policy. The existing policy is as follows:

> Declaration of Policy: The Board
>
> Sec. 102. In the exercise and performance of its powers and duties under this Act, the Board shall consider the following, among other things, as being in the public interest, and in accordance with the public convenience and necessity:
>
> (a) The encouragement and development of an air-transportation system properly adapted to the present and future needs of the foreign and domestic

commerce of the United States, of the Postal Service, and of the national defense:

(b) The regulation of air transportation in such manner as to recognize and preserve the inherent advantages of, assure the highest degree of safety in, and foster sound economic conditions in, such transportation, and to improve the relations between, and coordinate transportation by, air carriers:

(c) The promotion of adequate, economical, and efficient service by air carriers at reasonable charges, without unjust discriminations, undue preferences or advantages, or unfair or destructive competitive practices:

(d) Competition to the extent necessary to assure the sound development of an air-transportation system properly adapted to the needs of the foreign and domestic commerce of the United States, of the Postal Service, and of the national defense:

(e) The promotion of safety in air commerce: and

(f) The promotion, encouragement, and development of civil aeronautics.[3]

The Senate bill would replace this section of the Federal Aviation Act of 1958 with the following language:

Declaration of Policy: The Board
Interstate and Overseas Air Transportation

Sec. 102. (a) In the exercise and performance of its powers and duties under this Act with respect to interstate and overseas air transportation, the Board shall consider the following, among other things, as being in the public interest, and consistent with the public convenience and necessity:

(1) The maintenance and furtherance of a high degree of safety in air commerce.

(2) The development and maintenance of an efficient and reliable air transportation system which provides an opportunity for efficient and well-managed air carriers to earn a fair and reasonable return on investment in a competitive environment in order to meet the present and future needs of the public, the foreign and domestic commerce of the United States, the Postal Service, and the national defense.

(3) The encouragement, development, and maintenance of an air transportation system relying on actual and potential competition to provide efficiency, innovation and low prices, and to determine the variety, quality, and price of air transportation services.

(4) The creation, development, and maintenance of a sound regulatory and economic environment which facilitates entry into air transportation markets by new air carriers, and facilitates entry into additional air transportation markets by existing air carriers.

(5) The prevention of unfair, deceptive, predatory, or anticompetitive practices in air transportation, and the avoidance of (A) industry concentration, excessive market domination, monopoly power and (B) other conditions that would tend to allow one or more air carriers unreasonably to increase prices, reduce services, or exclude competition in air transportation.

(6) The maintenance of a comprehensive and convenient system of continuous scheduled airline service for small communities and for isolated areas, with direct Federal assistance where appropriate.

Foreign air transportation

(b) In the exercise and performance of its powers and duties under this Act with respect to foreign air transportation, the Board shall consider the following, among other things, as being in the public interest, and in accordance with the public convenience and necessity:

(1) The encouragement and development of an air transporation system properly adapted to the present and future needs of the foreign and domestic commerce of the United States, of the Postal Service, and of the national defense.

(2) The regulation of air transporation in such manner as to recognize and preserve the inherent advantages of, assure the highest degree of safety in, and foster sound economic conditions in such transportation, and to improve the relations between and coordinate transportation by air carriers.

(3) The promotion of adequate, economical, and efficient service by air carriers at reasonable charges, without unjust discriminations, undue preferences or advantages, or unfair or destructive competitive practices.

(4) Competition to the extent necessary to assure the sound development of an air transportation system properly adapted to the needs of the foreign and domestic commerce of the United States, of the Postal Service, and of the national defense.

(5) The promotion of safety in air commerce.

(6) The promotion, encouragement, and development of civil aeronautics.[4]

The declaration of policy contained in the House bill is as follows:

Declaration of Policy: The Board
Factors for Consideration

Sec. 102.(a)(1) In the exercise and performance of its powers and duties under this Act, the Board shall consider the following, among other things, as being in the public interest, and in accordance with the public convenience and necessity:

(A) The encouragement and development of an air transportation system which is responsive to the needs of the public and is adapted to the present and future needs of (i) the foreign and domestic commerce of the United States, (ii) the Postal Service, and (iii) the national defense.

(B) The availability of a variety of adequate, economic, efficient, and low-cost services by air carriers without unjust discriminations, undue preferences or advantages, or unfair or deceptive practices, and the need to improve relations among, and coordinate transportation by, air carriers.

(C) The placement of maximum reliance on competitive market forces and on actual and potential competition (i) to provide the needed air transportation system, and (ii) to encourage efficient and well-managed carriers to earn adequate profits and to attract capital.

(D) The encouragement of new air carriers.

(E) The importance of the highest degrees of safety in air commerce.

(2) In addition to the objectives set forth in paragraph (1) of this subsection, the Board, in the exercise and performance of its powers and duties under this

Act with respect to all-cargo air service shall consider the following, among other things, as being in the public interest.

(A) The encouragement and development of an expedited all-cargo air service system, provided by private enterprise, responsive to (i) the present and future needs of shippers, (ii) the commerce of the United States, and (iii) the national defense.

(B) The encouragement and development of an integrated transportation system relying upon competitive market forces to determine the extent, variety, quality, and price of such services.

(C) The provision of services without unjust discriminations, undue preferences or advantages, unfair or deceptive practices, or predatory pricing.

Air Carriers in Foreign Air Transportation

(b) In applying the policies described in subsection (a) of this section to air carriers engaging in foreign air transportation, the Board shall take into account any special factors or circumstances which it determines affect such transportation, including, but not limited to, circumstances under which—

(1) air carriers must compete primarily with foreign air carriers which are owned or financially supported by foreign governments;

(2) air carriers must operate under foreign laws and practices which limit and restrict their freedom to manage their operations with maximum efficiency;

(3) the extent of competition on foreign routes cannot be exclusively controlled by the Federal Government, but is determined through agreements with foreign governments;

(4) the level of service offered on foreign routes cannot be effectively adjusted to demand by reason of actions by foreign governments and basic characteristics of international air transport operations; and

(5) rates, fares, and charges cannot be established for any foreign route solely by the air carriers or the Federal Government, but must be approved by all the governments on the route.[5]

The declarations of policy in both bills clearly emphasize that the encouragement of competition is to be an important aspect of the CAB's regulatory responsibilities. There are certain differences, however, between the two proposed declarations of policy. The Senate version specifically states that the CAB is to maintain air service to small communities, using federal subsidies where appropriate. The House version does not include such a passage in its declaration of policy but addresses the issue in subsequent sections of the bill. Also, the Senate version retains the existing declaration of policy for foreign air transportation. In contrast, the House version applies the new declaration of policy to both interstate and foreign air transportation, noting that a number of special circumstances relating to foreign air transportation must be taken into account by the Board. It is not clear whether the Senate and House versions of the declaration of policy would have significantly different effects upon CAB regulation of the airline industry.

Certification of New Air Carriers

Existing Law	S. 2493	H.R. 8813
CAB shall certificate carriers which are fit, willing, and able, when required by the public convenience and necessity.	Certification shall occur when consistent with the public convenience and necessity. New types of service and lower fares are not inconsistent with the public interest.	Certification shall occur when consistent with the public convenience and necessity.

The present statutory authority of the CAB for certification of new air carriers is as follows: "No air carrier shall engage in any air transportation unless there is in force a certificate issued by the Board authorizing such air carrier to engage in such transportation. . . . The Board shall issue a certificate . . . if it finds that the applicant is fit, willing, and able to perform such transportation properly, . . . and that such transportation is required by the public convenience and necessity."[6] These criteria give the CAB a great deal of discretionary authority over the certification of air carriers. In the past, such authority has been used to limit entry severely, as noted in testimony by Secretary of Transportation Brock Adams:

> [W]e have found that since the original nineteen trunk carriers were grandfathered into the system there have been no new trunk carriers certified and the original nineteen have shrunk to eleven, including Pan Am. After World War II, a number of smaller feeder carriers, now known as the local service carriers, were allowed into the industry. Originally, there were nineteen of these carriers, but their number has also been reduced to eight. Although the local service carriers have grown to become "mini-trunks," they still only account for about 10 percent of domestic passenger travel. . . . In other words, there's been some entry, but not really enough.[7]

The Senate and the House bills are "aimed at relaxing the restrictions on the entry of new carriers by altering the criteria for certification." Thus, the Senate bill states that: "The Board shall issue a certificate . . . if the Board determines that . . . such air transportation is *consistent* with the public convenience and necessity" [emphasis added]. Furthermore, in determining whether the air transportation proposed "is consistent with the public convenience and necessity, the Board shall, in addition to the policy statement in Section 102(a) of this Act [the declaration of policy], be guided as follows: Innovative or more efficient methods of operation in air transportation, or significant reductions in fares . . . are consistent with the public convenience and necessity. The avoidance of industry concentration, excessive market domination, monopoly power and other conditions [allowing] carriers to increase prices, reduce services, or exclude competition . . . is consistent with the public convenience and necessity. The diversion of revenue or traffic from another carrier is not in itself inconsistent with the public convenience and necessity."[8]

The House bill also alters the criteria for awarding certificates by changing the clause "is required by the public convenience and necessity" to "is consistent with the public convenience and necessity."[9] However, it does not elaborate on the meaning of "the public convenience and necessity." The bill does direct that the Board "shall promulgate rules establishing simplified procedures for the disposition of applications for a certificate to engage in air transportation."[10] The simplified procedures to be used are not specified. Thus, the Senate version is more specific with respect to the certification of new air carriers. It not only alters the criteria for certification, but defines these criteria as well. The House version lacks such specific definitions of the public convenience and necessity, leaving such judgments to the discretion of the Board. Consequently, the Senate version would probably be more effective in encouraging the certification of new air carriers.

Proponents of deregulation argue that the entry of new carriers is necessary to ensure that airline markets are competitive. By denying applications for certificates, the CAB has excluded new firms which have offered lower fares and/or improved air service. Also, the mere threat of entry is often sufficient to induce existing firms to lower prices, increase service quality, or improve efficiency. In many cases, applications were rejected for fear that the new competition would weaken existing carriers. Therefore, those in favor of easier entry would tend to prefer the Senate bill, since it specifically instructs the CAB as to the proper interpretation of "the public convenience and necessity." This amendment, if adopted, is expected to result in the approval of a number of applications for new certificates.

Opponents of deregulation argue that the entry of new carriers will exacerbate the problems of cutthroat competition and predatory practices. New entrants are considered to be especially likely to instigate rounds of destructive price competition as they attempt to establish themselves on new routes. This could lead to prolonged losses for all carriers offering air service in such markets. Furthermore, new carriers will probably first challenge the routes of the weaker existing carriers, perhaps by using predatory tactics. If successful, the weak carriers will be driven out of their markets, and perhaps into bankruptcy. Thus, opponents contend, permitting new entry is likely to lead to new carriers replacing old, with no net increase in the number of airlines.

New Routes for Existing Carriers

Existing Law	S. 2493	H.R. 8813
Existing carriers must apply for new route authority under the same provisions as those governing certification of new air carriers.	CAB shall grant route authority to additional carriers on those routes with unused authority. Also, subject to certain limitations, each carrier may select up to two new routes each year for which it will obtain certification.	CAB shall grant route authority to additional carriers on those routes with unused authority. Also, subject to certain limitations, each carrier may select one new route each year for which it will obtain certification.

Under present statutes, there are no specialized procedures to deal with existing carriers who wish to obtain new routes. Such air carriers must make application for expanded route authority in the same manner as new firms apply for certification, by demonstrating that they are fit, willing, and able to provide the service in question. In practice, permission to serve new air routes is often denied, typically for the same reasons used to reject new entrants to the industry. The Senate and the House bills contain specific provisions regarding the granting of new routes to existing carriers. Both bills differentiate between two types of routes: (1) those on which one or more carriers are not using their present route authority; and (2) other routes.

The Senate bill first addresses those routes which fall into category (1).

> Any carrier holding a certificate . . . may file an application with the Board seeking authority to provide nonstop scheduled air transportation between two points listed on a certificate issued . . . to any other carrier. The Board shall award such authority to the applicant air carrier, if the Board determines that . . . such other air carrier has not exercised such authority . . . at a minimum 5 round trips per week for at least 180 days during the 12 months immediately preceding the date on which such application was filed.[11]

The House bill contains similar provisions regarding routes in category (1).

> If an air carrier is authorized by its certificate to provide round trip service nonstop each way between any two points in interstate air transportation and such air carrier fails to provide such service on 180 days or more during any calendar year. . . , upon application, the Board shall . . . issue a certificate to an applicant . . . who is fit, willing, and able to provide such round trip nonstop service . . . (except that) not more than one certificate shall be issued . . . for round trip nonstop service between two points . . . based on the failure of the same carrier to provide such service between such two points.[12]

Thus, the significant difference between the Senate and the House versions concerns the minimum levels of service that carriers must provide in order to avoid new entry on their routes. The Senate bill requires five round trips per week for 180 days during any twelve month period. The House bill specifies a minimum of 180 days of service during each calendar year. It is unclear which provision will be more stringent in establishing minimum levels of air service.

The legislative treatment of routes in category (2) is substantially different. The general provisions of the Senate bill are as follows. Each interstate or intrastate carrier may select two new routes each year for which it will be granted a temporary certificate. In order to qualify, a carrier must have operated more than 125 million available-seat-miles during the preceding twelve months, and the total length of the two routes chosen must not exceed 3,000 miles. A temporary certificate will be issued unless a route chosen has been closed to new entry, or the CAB finds that the carrier "is not fit, willing, and able to provide the air transportation selected."[13] Each year, a carrier may designate a number of its routes as being closed to new entry, such number declining from three in 1979 to none after 1983. For the years 1979–1981, there are further restrictions as to the total number of its routes on which a carrier must face new entry. The temporary certificates issued under these provisions would become permanent after the new entrant has operated regularly scheduled nonstop service for eighteen consecutive months.

The House bill deals with category (2) routes in much the same manner, with certain exceptions. Intrastate carriers will be eligible to select new routes if their available-seat-miles during the preceding twelve months exceeded 100 million. Carriers may select only one new route each year, regardless of its length. No more than one new carrier will be permitted to enter any route during a three-year period. Carriers would not have the right to designate certain of their routes as being closed to new entry. Finally, the bill contains provisions allowing certificated foreign carriers to obtain a limited number of domestic routes: "any air carrier holding a valid certificate to engage in foreign air transportation may apply . . . to provide passenger or cargo service, or both, between points in the United States between which it is authorized to operate while engaging in foreign air transportation."[14] Such carriers would be restricted to two new routes per year (three in the first year), and may not provide more than one flight per day in each direction on each such route. In summary, certain provisions of the Senate bill are more conducive to new entry than the corresponding passages of the House bill, while in other provisions, the House version is more accommodating to new entrants.

Arguments for and against the certification of new carriers, presented in the preceding section, apply as well to the granting of new routes to existing carriers. Opponents offer the further argument that such new entry will sharply reduce the profitability of a carrier's prized routes because such routes will be among the first chosen for new entry. Without the sizable profits contributed by these desirable routes, it is argued, carriers will be more likely to abandon their service on marginal or unprofitable routes, and many communities will lose air service. C. E. Meyer, Jr., president of Trans World Airlines testified in regard to S. 292 and S. 689, predecessors of S. 2493, that:

> [I]f you bring in competition and the attack is on those major transcontinental routes and semi-transcontinental routes, the denser routes, and you undermine the profitability of those, then the economics is no longer there for serving those smaller communities. Each of the major carriers maintains route segment profitability systems. We can bring stacks of them . . . and show you that those small segments lose money. They make money when they interconnect with the longer routes . . . [Also, the] massive entry into those smaller markets—which, by the way, have fairly high load factors, many of them—would tend to fractionate the market to where two carriers could not make a profit out of it.[15]

Proponents argue there is no evidence that a significant amount of cross-subsidization takes place. That is, profits on some routes are not used to support air service on other routes. Senator Kennedy has stated:

> There is no evidence to support the myth that airlines are providing significant money-losing service to small communities that is subsidized by highly profitable operations where the CAB protects them from competition. The dense and most popular markets are already quite competitive and the two, three, or more carriers serving them generate little or no "excess" profit that these same carriers use to service towns they would prefer not to serve. The fact is that

> CAB regulations positively discourage this kind of cross-subsidy . . . and, though some airlines continue to allege that substantial cross-subsidy exists and is responsible for providing service to small communities, they have been unable to present any evidence to support the claims.[16]

In any case, the argument continues, carriers will always have an incentive to abandon unprofitable air routes, whether or not they face new entrants in their highly profitable markets. Thus, increased entry would not threaten small communities with the loss of air service.

Flexibility in Air Fares

Existing Law	S. 2493	H.R. 8813
CAB has the authority to reject any tariff, giving it control over all air fares.	CAB, under most circumstances, cannot reject proposed fares unless they are more than 5 percent above or 35 percent below standard industry fare levels.	CAB, under most circumstances, cannot reject proposed fares unless they are more than (a) 10 percent above the year-earlier fare, or (b) 25 percent below the lowest fare in effect on the date of enactment (50 percent after the first year following enactment).

Under present statutes, the CAB "is empowered to reject any tariff [and] any tariff so rejected shall be void."[17] In exercising and performing its powers and duties with respect to the determination of rates, "the Board shall take into consideration, among other factors . . . [t]he need in the public interest of adequate and efficient transportation of persons and property by air carriers at the lowest cost consistent with the furnishing of such service; . . . [t]he need of each air carrier for revenue sufficient to enable such air carrier, under honest, economical, and efficient management to provide adequate and efficient air carrier service."[18]

The Senate and House bills are aimed at reducing the CAB's control over air fares. The House version states that "the Board shall take into consideration, among other factors . . . the desirability of a variety of price and service options such as peak and off-peak pricing or other pricing mechanisms to improve economic efficiency and provide low-cost air service; and the desirability of allowing an air carrier to determine prices in response to particular competitive market conditions on the basis of such air carrier's individual cost."[19]

Furthermore, the House version says:

> [t]he Board shall not have authority to find any rate, fare, or charge for interstate air transportation of persons, to be unjust or unreasonable . . . if (A) with respect to any proposed increase, such proposed . . . charge would not be

> more than 10 percentum higher than the . . . charge in effect one year prior . . . for the same class of service . . . (B) with respect to any proposed decrease filed within one year after the date of enactment of this paragraph, the proposed . . . charge would not be more than 25 percentum lower than the lowest charge in effect on such date of enactment for the same class of service . . . or (C) with respect to any proposed decrease filed (later than one year after enactment) . . . such proposed . . . charge would not be more than the lesser of (i) 50 percentum lower than the lowest . . . charge in effect on the date of enactment . . . for the same class of service . . . or, (ii) 110 percentum of the direct costs of the carrier in providing the service.[20]

The Senate bill, adopting a similar approach to fare regulation, states that:

> [t]he Board may not (A) determine any fare . . . charged . . . by an air carrier for interstate . . . scheduled air transportation of persons (other than a fare . . . charged . . . by an air carrier . . . in any city pair market in which the air carrier transports 70 percent or more of the passenger air traffic . . .) to be unjust or unreasonable on the basis that it is too high, unless after July 1, 1979, the fare is . . . more than 5 percent higher than the standard industry fare level for the same or essentially similar class of service . . . (B) determine any fare . . . charged . . . to be unjust or unreasonable on the basis that it is too low, unless the fare is (i) . . . more than 35 percent below the standard industry fare level for the same or essentially similar class of service; or (ii) predatory.[21]

Furthermore, the Senate bill says, "the party opposing any fare or charge on the basis that it is too low shall have the burden of proving that the fare or charge is too low."[22]

The main differences between the House and the Senate bills are in the upper and lower bounds within which air fares would be permitted to move freely. The House version appears to allow for greater fare flexibility. The Senate version has two provisions not found in the House bill: (1) the CAB could suspend any fare which it determined to be predatory, even if such fare were to be within the permissible bounds; and (2) the burden of proof would lie with any party opposing a low fare.

Opponents argue that flexible air fares will lead to cutthroat competition and predatory pricing, as discussed below. In addition, as air fares are reduced, service quality will decline as carriers attempt to avert losses on their routes. Thus, consumers will be saddled with inferior air service, and the air transportation network may be harmed.

Proponents argue that price flexibility is necessary to allow efficient firms to pass cost savings along to consumers. Furthermore, when air carriers compete in both price and service quality, travelers can decide whether such factors as frequent flights and spacious aircraft seating are worth their cost. At present, consumers have no choice but to pay for the high levels of service quality being provided.

Reduction or Suspension of Air Service

Existing Law	S. 2493	H.R. 8813
No carrier may terminate air service unless the CAB finds it to be in the public interest.	No carrier may terminate service without 90 days notice; CAB may delay such termination for up to 90 days and may grant subsidies to certified carriers to maintain essential air service.	No carrier may terminate service without 90 days notice; CAB may delay such termination for up to 270 days and may grant subsidies to commuter air carriers to maintain essential air service.

Under present statutes, no air carrier "shall abandon any route, or part thereof, for which a certificate has been issued by the Board, unless, upon the application of such air carrier, after notice and hearing, the Board shall find such abandonment to be in the public interest."[23] Route abandonment is seldom permitted because, although it may be in a carrier's interest, it can rarely be shown to be in the public interest. Currently, annual subsidies are paid to most local-service carriers by the CAB. They are granted so that carriers can offer air service to small communities which could not be served by certificated carriers on a profitable basis. These subsidies are awarded to each airline on the basis of its systemwide operating costs and revenues.

The Senate and the House bills would establish new procedures to deal with route abandonment. The House bill states that no air carrier "shall terminate any service required by its certificate of public convenience and necessity unless it has filed with the Board and served upon each community directly affected by such termination notice of the proposed termination at least ninety days before the date such service is to be terminated. . . . Before the end of the notice period . . . the Board may, upon complaint or upon its own initiative, delay the termination of the service . . . for a period of not more than 270 days from the date of the proposed termination in order to allow arrangements to be made for substitute service."[24] In addition, the CAB would be given the authority to grant subsidies when necessary to maintain essential air service whenever the Board determines that: "(A) the public interest requires interstate air transportation for persons, property, or mail between two or more points . . . which do not receive certificated air carrier service, and (B) no adequate service will be provided by any air carrier or commuter air carrier between such points without federal financial assistance, the Board may establish a rate of compensation to be paid for providing such service to that commuter air carrier which by order of the Board provides such service."[25] Such subsidies will be granted, however, on a route, rather than on a systemwide, basis. That is, the amount of compensation will depend upon the costs and revenues associated with the provision of essential air service on each route.

The Senate bill contains almost identical provisions, except, the Board may delay the termination of service for a period of not more than ninety days. Also, air carriers eligible to provide essential air service under subsidy are the domestic trunk carriers and the local service carriers.

It has been argued that the commuter air carriers will be more efficient than the trunk or local service carriers in providing subsidized air service. This is due to the extensive experience of the former group in low density air markets, as well as their use of smaller aircraft more appropriate to such markets. Consequently it is argued that the House bill is to be preferred, since it directs the CAB to provide subsidized service through the use of commuter air carriers.

Opponents of the bills argue that permitting the abandonment of routes will result in the disruption of air service to many communities. Even when substitute service is arranged, with or without subsidy, there will be a transition period with uncertainty concerning such matters as fares and flight schedules.

Proponents of the bills argue that carriers must be free to exit from markets when their resources can be used more effectively on other routes. Proponents argue further that the bills ensure that essential air service will be provided on a continuous basis.

ARGUMENTS FOR AND AGAINST DEREGULATION

Airline deregulation advocates argue that the course of action they propose would lead to a more efficient air transportation system, characterized by a mix of fares and air services which consumers would prefer to those under the present system. Opponents argue that airline deregulation would severely damage our extensive air transportation network—one which almost everyone agrees is the best in the world. Specific aspects of this argument, pro and con, are presented below.

Variety of Services Offered

At present, all air fares are subject to CAB approval. Existing procedures and criteria tend to restrict airline experimentation with novel services and fares which travelers might prefer. Senator Kennedy, a supporter of regulatory reform, has stated:

> Although today's regulatory system does sometimes allow certain types of discount fares provided they are restricted and limited in a variety of ways, there is no compelling public policy reason why the Federal Government should prevent airline companies from lowering their fares generally, or experimenting with cheaper coach seats on some of its routes.[26]

In an unregulated market, the argument goes, new types of services would be provided whenever an opportunity arises to offer them profitably. The intrastate air carriers have been cited as proof of this proposition. These carriers are subject to state regulation on intrastate routes, but are not subject to CAB rate and entry control on interstate routes. As an example of the experimental service that could occur in an unregulated market, Pacific Southwest Airlines for a number of years offered travelers on certain routes in California a choice between propeller and jet service. High-seating-density/low-fare air service continues to be offered to consumers in those markets. In Texas, Southwest Airlines has adopted an innovative fare structure, charging very low prices to off-peak travelers.[27]

Opponents of deregulation argue that present air fares are low by any reasonable standards. In addition, air carriers compete by improving service quality—for example, more frequent flights, more comfortable aircraft, and better meals. This increased quality directly benefits air travelers. In an unregulated environment, consumers would obtain lower fares only by enduring cramped seating in crowded aircraft cabins, with infrequent departures. Furthermore, cost savings under deregulation would prove illusory, it is argued. Carriers would be no more successful at resisting cost increases than they have been under CAB regulation. Thus, lower air fares would only result in inferior air services.

Costs of Operation and Fares

At present, the CAB determines which carriers may operate on each route and what fares they may charge. Thus, the airlines can compete for passengers only by increasing their flight frequency, improving their flight scheduling, expanding their meal service, or adding other amenities. These limited forms of competition raise the carriers' operating costs, primarily by reducing aircraft passenger load factors. The increased numbers of empty seats must be paid for, resulting in higher air fares. Again, the intrastate carriers are cited. Their load factors are consistently higher and their fares consistently lower than on comparable interstate routes subject to CAB regulation.[28] By permitting price competition, proponents argue, deregulation would lead to more efficient use of aircraft capacity, resulting in lower costs and lower air fares. Charles Schultze, chairman of the Council of Economic Advisers, has stated that:

> the way airline fares can be brought down is by putting more seats in planes and by filling these seats. Wages don't have to be cut. Fuel prices don't have to fall. And safety doesn't have to be compromised by cutting maintenance expenditures.[29]

Similarly, Senator Kennedy has testified that:

> The fact is that current regulation brings about its own peculiar form of wasteful competition, and it exacts a fearsome cost. . . . The airlines channel their competitive energies into costlier service and chase the travel dollars with frills and lavish scheduling which sends planes off across the country half empty. . . . It explains why airline prices can be too high at the very same time airline profits are too low.[30]

Under the present regulatory system, fare increases are usually approved when carriers' costs increase. This, proponents argue, provides little incentive for the airlines to control rising costs, since to a certain extent these can be passed along to passengers. In an unregulated environment, a carrier would attempt to stem rising costs, since these would place the carrier at a competitive disadvantage in regard to other airlines. Thus, the airlines should tend to incur lower costs in the absence of CAB regulation. Frederick Stevenson, assistant professor of transportation and business logistics at Northeastern University, has stated:

> The facts are that most consumers are paying prices too high because airline productivity is too low and costs are too inflated. . . . Additionally, costs are too high because airline employees are overpaid. . . . Present regulations are the cause of this problem, for they discourage rate competition, they do not allow low-cost carriers to enter the industry, and they do not let inefficient firms fail.[31]

Deregulation opponents counter that these are purely theoretical arguments that ignore the reality of the airline business. This argument has been articulated by R. S. Maurer, senior vice president of Delta Air Lines:

> Another argument of the ardent reformers is that airline prices in this country are too high, and that the basic reason is insufficient price competition. Again,

historic and present fact contradict these assertions. The existing statute does in fact provide for considerable airline rate and fare competition and there has been and is a great deal of it. . . . Not only does the current statute provide for price competition, with the result that there has been much of it, but it is equally important to recognize that the United States has long enjoyed the lowest fares for scheduled airline service of any area on earth. . . . airline fares in the United States are generally at least 30 percent lower than fares in Europe. In many instances, they are as much as 50 percent lower. And this is not a new situation. Over the years the airlines have done nothing short of a miraculous job holding rates and fares down. Indeed, from 1950 to 1976 the Consumer Price Index, reflecting primarily prices from the unregulated sectors of the economy, rose 136 percent, while air fares rose less than 40 percent! . . . The record is plain: The scheduled airline industry has done a *better* job over the years than most manufacturing and service companies in holding the price of its service down, and its prices today are lower than the prices for comparable service anywhere else on earth. . . . Even if we were able to have total deregulation, which everyone agrees is wrong, still: The price of jet fuel would not go down. Skilled airline employees would not work for less. Airport operators would not lower their landing fees. Nor would other suppliers of goods and services to the airlines lower their prices. . . . [Some critics have not] attempted to evaluate the additional cost of inconvenience to individual travelers—such as the impact of higher load factors, denser seating and possibly less timely flights. . . . [Proposals for lower fares may call for] too much sacrifice of passenger convenience, lauding a sort of "cattle car" service which, in some areas, helped kill railroad passenger service and even adversely affected earlier airline service on certain monopoly routes.[32]

Fares and Profits

At present, carriers may not serve new air routes or lower their fares without CAB approval. In practice, new route authority is seldom granted, and general fare cuts and new discount fares are frequently rejected. Thus, a carrier's attempts to improve air service by operating a new route or lowering fares are usually thwarted. In an unregulated environment, however, carriers could enter new markets or reduce fares at will. The competitive process would drive fares down to the level that corresponds to the costs of efficient carriers.[33] If an airline attempted to charge excessive fares and thereby achieve monopoly profits, new carriers could enter the market and undercut the high fares. Insufficient profits would result only for those carriers which operate inefficiently, thus providing an incentive to improve airline management. Representative Millicent Fenwick (R-N.J.), a supporter of regulatory reform, testified that reducing CAB control over fares and entry would have the following results:

> It will enable carriers to better tailor their services to consumer needs and public interest. And it [new entry] will police the new pricing flexibility, since carriers will have less incentive to cut [ticket] costs drastically to drive out competitors, knowing that competitors can reenter if fares return to higher levels. They also will have less incentive to raise prices above competitive levels, knowing that potential entrants will eagerly enter the market to com-

pete. The result should be a more healthy and competitive environment, in which resources will be allocated based on truer competitive advantage and where carriers can adjust services and realign markets as economic conditions warrant. The benefits which result from an atmosphere of vigorous competition are clearly in the public interest.[34]

If this result were certain, those against deregulation would probably drop their opposition on this point at least. Opponents argue, however, that the lower fares may force weaker carriers into bankruptcy, creating airline monopolies. This argument has been expressed by Lee West, a member of the Civil Aeronautics Board:

> One of my chief concerns is that an abrupt relaxation of controls could lead to a heavy concentration within the industry—a domination by the larger and better financed carriers, who would have the resources and flexibility to drive smaller carriers out of the system and to keep out would-be entrants. The combination of sheer size and pricing freedom could give large carriers a powerful weapon to increase their dominance, if allowed free entry into the markets of a small competitor.[35]

Route Reductions

Proponents of deregulation argue that few cities would lose air service completely. In cases where CAB-certificated carriers do abandon markets, commuter air carriers have often provided comparable air transportation on a profitable basis. As Senator Kennedy has stated:

> Some factions of the aviation industry have tried to spread the notion that less regulation will result in substantial loss of service. This notion is simply false and should be laid to rest. . . . [It is a] myth that the Board's conventional price and entry regulations somehow guarantee service to small communities. They do no such thing. The Board is prohibited by law from controlling either equipment or schedules, so has virtually no control over how a town is served, either in terms of frequency or timing. And, it seldom requires that a particular route be flown. The restrictions the Board places on airline operating authority are primarily designed to keep competition out of protected markets, rather than compel service that would not otherwise be provided. . . . In addition, the present system of economic regulation has allowed the cessation of certificated service to many small communities. The Board has been quite liberal in allowing airlines to drop unprofitable points. In the last fifteen years, 170 points have lost certificated air service, an amount equal to nearly one-third of the points previously served. . . . Although Board regulation did not maintain air service to those 170 communities, unregulated commuter carriers voluntarily serve nearly 100 of those towns today. . . . The commuter carriers operating in an unregulated environment guarantee better than do CAB rules stable, high-quality, convenient service to small communities.[36]

In economic terms, proponents contend, when demand is insufficient to cover costs of air service, it may be difficult to justify such service. Furthermore, higher load factors do not necessarily imply reductions in flight frequency, since lower fares could well attract large numbers of new air passengers on most routes.

Opponents argue that as competition causes air fares to fall, carriers would have to compensate by raising load factors on teir aircraft. This would mean a reduction in flight frequency on many routes. Along with the reduction in the total number of flights, the air transportation network would shrink. Airline passengers would suffer increasing delays, especially when using connecting flights. In an unregulated environment, carriers, free to abandon unprofitable routes, would eliminate scheduled air service to many small communities, causing inconvenience, hardship, and economic loss to their citizens. As R. S. Maurer has argued:

> We would state our deep concern that fully adequate small community service be retained. Proper service to and from small communities, and in small markets, is already part of the rationalized system which we think is so important and beneficial to the United States traveling and shipping public, and the United States Postal Service. We are also firmly convinced that excessive regulatory reform, particularly any significant provision for freedom of entry into and from air transportation markets, would considerably weaken small community service and lead to the abandonment of much of that service as we know it today.[37]

Competition, Predatory Practices, and Monopoly Control

Proponents of deregulation contend that price competition presents a danger of instability only if airline managements are willing to provide air service at prices below their costs—an unlikely proposition. Predatory tactics are sensible only if a carrier cannot reenter a market once it is driven out. Otherwise, a monopoly can never be established by an aggressive carrier because in a deregulated environment, firms could enter new markets or reenter old markets at will, aided by the most mobile capital good known—the modern jet aircraft. Finally, large carriers could drive their smaller rivals out of markets only if large carriers had a cost advantage over small carriers. Evidence indicates, however, that there are no significant economies of scale in airline operation, so large and small carriers could compete on an equal basis. Donald Baker, former assistant attorney general for antitrust, has testified that:

> We believe the key to preventing predatory behavior is not regulatory control of fares, but a policy of liberal entry and pricing. Predatory pricing is not profitable unless the predator is able to raise prices after it has driven its competitors out of the market. But if the predator knows its rivals can reappear simply by routing airplanes to the market and selling tickets, it will see that exploitation of the monopoly position is impossible. Economists have concluded that the prospects for profitable predatory conduct are poor in unregulated air transport markets. I would say parenthetically that regulation can increase the problems of predation. . . . Moreover, the "natural monopoly" argument, which some advance to justify economic regulation, finds no support in the facts of air transportation economics. The larger air carriers do

> not enjoy "economies of scale"; that is, any cost advantages the largest air carriers may enjoy because of their large size are more than offset by the increased costs and inflexibilities of managing a large complex and dynamic airline system. In addition, the most costly air carrier assets are much more highly mobile than the key assets of, for instance, oil pipelines or electrical generating plants. Aircraft are adaptable to a variety of uses, and are easily shifted from markets of low demand to markets of high demand.[38]

Opponents argue that this is an unrealistic view. In an unregulated market, airlines would compete primarily by reducing air fares. No carrier would permit its fares to be undercut, for fear of losing its passengers to rival carriers. Hence, fares would spiral downward as each airline attempted to gain a competitive advantage. Ultimately, this cutthroat competition would cause all the carriers to charge fares below their operating costs, and all would suffer financial losses. This would clearly damage the air transportation network. Furthermore, an aggressive carrier might intentionally instigate such a price war as a predatory tactic. By causing its rivals to incur losses, it might be able to force them to abandon certain routes, or even drive them to bankruptcy. The aggressor, with financial reserves to weather such losses, might then be able to establish a monopoly. This position is argued by Gerald O'Grady, senior vice president-legal of Western Air Lines, in testimony concerning fare flexibility:

> We object to carriers being given discretion to increase or decrease fares or rates in individual markets subject only to the restriction that such fares or rates shall not fall below "direct costs.". . . This provision in effect authorizes the carriers to engage in rate wars in individual markets, with the one which can best afford to lose money being ultimately successful in driving competitors out of the market. . . . [W]e say that this provision authorizes predatory pricing leading inevitably to rate wars in which only the richest can survive. The small carrier under this form of regulation does not stand a chance.[39]

In the absence of CAB regulation, opponents contend, the larger carriers would expand to serve all the profitable air routes. In the process, they would drive out the smaller carriers, allowing the latter to operate only in unprofitable markets. The large firms would then establish monopolies or oligopolies on most routes, charging excessive fares to air travelers. Thus, economic regulation by the CAB is necessary to prevent the large carriers from dominating the air transportation network and exploiting consumers. A joint statement of the Airport Operators Council International and American Association of Airport Executives argues:

> Airports are concerned that excessive competitive freedom could result in rapidly shifting air service patterns and a decline in the quality of air service to the public. In major markets, over-competition could occur as carriers attempt to utilize their resources where there is the greatest potential for profit. Should this happen, such markets could experience over-capacity, lower load factors, and reduced market shares for each carrier. The immediate result may be that formerly choice, profitable markets could become unprofitable. Such over-competition could eventually lead to the dominance of a small number of carriers and the decline of competition, to the detriment of the public interest.[40]

Safety

Proponents of deregulation note that air safety regulation is the responsibility of the Federal Aviation Administration, not the CAB. Proposals to eliminate or reform airline regulation are all aimed at CAB economic regulation, not FAA safety regulation. Hence, air safety will be unaffected. This position is taken by Richard Ferris, president of United Airlines, a supporter of regulatory reform:

> [It is argued that] weak profit performance by airlines can prompt corner-cutting in maintenance, thereby making airlines less safe. That really irks me. First, United isn't supporting regulatory reform because we think it will make airlines less profitable—quite the contrary. Second, no proposal has been made that in any way would change safety regulation by the Federal Aviation Administration. If there is any concrete basis whatever for the assertion that regulatory reform will impair air safety, I, for one, would like to know what it is.[41]

Opponents counter that this argument ascribes an unlikely omniscience to FAA safety regulation. Without CAB price regulation, carriers would engage in fare cutting as a form of competition. In order to maintain their profitability, airlines would be forced to reduce costs. This might lead to skimping on aircraft maintenance and safety margins. Consequently, the safety of the traveling public might be jeopardized. William Mahoney, counsel to the Air Line Pilots Association, has stated that:

> If the representatives of the employees in this industry are experts on anything, it is safety. Thanks to their strenuous efforts, often alone and often together with management, this nation can boast the world's safest air service. But employees know the effects upon safety of carrier employers having to cut corners in order to survive, as for example in the astounding number of train derailments throughout the United States. Every instinct tells us that the rail safety record will be repeated in the air transport industry as air carriers feel compelled to cut corners in order to stay in business.[42]

CONCLUSION

Some version of airline regulatory reform may well be voted this session of Congress or the next. The measure has the support of President Carter, important congressional leaders, the academic community, and the press.

The initiative to reform airline regulation is related to another issue also before this Congress—namely, how the airlines will meet the new noise standards promulgated by the Environmental Protection Agency and the Federal Aviation Administration. These agencies require that over the next few years the U.S. airlines meet more stringent requirements concerning the noise emitted by the aircraft they operate. To meet such standards, in some instances the airlines will have to buy new, quieter aircraft and sell off their noisier planes; in other cases, the airlines may choose to "retrofit" existing aircraft, which requires certain engine modifications. The expenditures involved are very large, ranging in the hundreds of millions of dollars per year.

To meet these new regulations, the airlines are asking for federal help. Basically, they see two problems. One is simply financing the retrofit or the purchase of new aircraft. The second is that the impact on the airlines will vary according to individual aircraft fleets. Airlines that have noisier fleets are asking for some mechanism to "share" the cost burden over the whole industry. One program that has received attention would use part of the money in the airport and airway development fund (collected primarily from an 8 percent tax on passenger tickets) for retrofitting and for the purchase of quieter aircraft.

According to press reports, any bill to reform airline regulations will probably also contain provisions aiding the airlines to meet the noise standards. In this respect, airline regulatory reform would be much like railroad reform (Railroad Revitalization and Regulatory Reform Act of 1976) in which legislation to reduce Interstate Commerce Commission regulation over railroad rates was combined with legislation establishing Conrail to revitalize the bankrupt railroads in the northeastern part of the country.

NOTES TO TEXT

[1]Public Law 85-726, "Federal Aviation Act of 1958," section 102 (cited hereafter as P.L. 85-726).

[2]The Federal Aviation Agency was established in 1958. In 1966, it was renamed the Federal Aviation Administration and was made a part of the newly created Department of Transportation.

[3]P.L. 85-726, section 102.

[4]U.S. Congress, Senate, S. 2493, 95th Congress, 1st session, 1977, section 2 (cited hereafter as S. 2493).

[5]U.S. Congress, House, H.R. 8813, 95th Congress, 1st session, 1977, section 2 (cited hereafter as H.R. 8813).

[6]P.L. 85-726, section 401.

[7]U.S. Congress, Senate, Subcommittee on Aviation of the Committee on Commerce, Science, and Transportation, *Hearings on S. 292 and S. 689,* 95th Congress, 1st session, 1977, part 3, p. 1366 (cited hereafter as *Hearings*).

[8]S. 2493, section 5.

[9]H.R. 8813, section 5.

[10]H.R. 8813, section 12.

[11]S. 2493, section 5.

[12]H.R. 8813, section 6.

[13]S. 2493, section 5.

[14]H.R. 8813, section 7.

[15]*Hearings,* part 1, p. 473.

[16]Ibid., p. 109.

[17]P.L. 85-726, section 403.

[18]Ibid., section 1002.

[19]H.R. 8813, section 23.

[20]Ibid.

[21]S. 2493, section 18.

[22]Ibid.

[23]P.L. 85-726, section 401.

[24]H.R. 8813, section 11.

[25]Ibid., section 19.

[26]*Hearings,* part 1, p. 100.

[27]For a description of the experiences of the intrastate air carriers, see "An Analysis of the Intrastate Air Carrier Regulatory Forum: Volume I/Summary Report," prepared for the Air Transportation Policy Staff, Office of the Secretary, U.S. Department of Transportation by Simat, Helliesen & Eichner, Inc., 1976.

[28]See, for example, Theodore E. Keeler, "Airline Regulation and Market Performance," *Bell Journal of Economics,* Autumn 1972, pp. 399-424.

[29]*Hearings,* part 1, p. 254.

[30]Ibid., p. 101.

[31]Ibid., p. 318.

[32]Ibid., part 2, pp. 889-895.

[33]See, for example, George C. Eads, "Competition in the Domestic Trunk Airline Industry: Too Much or Too Little?" in *Promoting Competition in Regulated Markets,* ed. Almarin Phillips (Washington, D.C.: The Brookings Institution, 1975), pp. 13-54.

[34]*Hearings,* part 3, p. 1462.

[35]Ibid., part 1, p. 135.

[36]Ibid., pp. 108-109.

[37]Ibid., part 2, p. 923.

[38]Ibid., pp. 571-572.

[39]Ibid., part 3, pp. 1374, 1382.

[40]Ibid., p. 1429.

[41]Letter to the Editor, *Fortune,* October 1977, p. 115.

[42]*Hearings,* part 3, p. 1286.